THE DREAM OF SNOWY OWLS

MONTY REID

Longspoon Press

Canadian Cataloguing in Publication Data

Reid, Monty, 1952 -
    The dream of snowy owls

Poems.
ISBN 0-919285-17-1

I. Title.
PS8585.E43D7   C811'.54   C83-091163-4
PR9199.3.R43D7

The Dream of Snowy Owls has been set in Baskerville
    10 - point type.

Longspoon Press
c/o Department of English
University of Alberta
Edmonton, Alberta T6G 2E5

Books may be ordered from your bookstore or directly
    from Longspoon Press.

Credits:
Editing for the Press: *Douglas Barbour and Paul Hjartarson*
Cover design: *Jorge Frascara*
Paste up: *Jane Edwards*
Typesetting: *May Chung*
Printing: *Hignell Printing, Winnipeg*
Financial Assistance: *Alberta Culture*
                              The Canada Council

For Pat

Acknowledgements

I would like to thank the editors of the following journals, in which these poems first appeared: *The Capilano Review, Descant, Event, Writ.* And thank you to the Canada Council.

Table of contents

January

i

Traffic advisory

yesterday, a chinook with rain
and today, a sharp freeze

glare ice, at intersections the
lights gradually disappear, illusory,

the exhaust full of a necessary
traffic, the cycle of arched cloud,
air full of glass, ice

fog, as your breath, at the
window, transforms it

ii

Thermostat

small things: glass
    blooms, curtains
    swell with air, a
    spring tightens on the wall

she stands on a register in
front of the window and
waits for the heat to go on

outside
       it hurts to breathe

and where she stands, imperceptibly,
air
      bends steel

iii

The chimes

Beneath the rigid streetlamps, a cold
haze, and here, Corey talks in his sleep.

He is restless and I have never understood
him.   The lights hum,

facetted, and beneath them a swarm
of crystal, the air glowing, static.

And it is too late for any movement
on the street except wind

swaying in the new tubular chimes our
neighbours hung above their door.   Soft

metal.   Inaudible, the wind not
enough to sound them, not enough

to shift the haze.
There is only the furnace, here,

regulated into flame, its breath
conducted as simply

through the house as the chimes
conduct air around them and

Corey, talking, the street
light through his window, kicking

the covers silently
off.

iv

The drift

that the wind between these houses
fills with glass, snow swept
from other roofs, the garage, the
deck built last summer

that glass, at the corner, curves
over beds of brittle cedar, foundation
plantings, shrubs along the walk
and stops, totally

except to settle, as you do into
sleep, into a compact dream, that I
watch the snow form, its lost
delicacy

as it is composed, wound
among twigs of a small nanking
cherry, planted too late
in the season

v

R-value

spun glass, separate fibre upon
fibre, glass full of air

as this room is filled with intricate
flesh, moonlight

sifting, glass in the cloud
caught in pockets of dead

air, the exchange of nothing
save desire

across the insular, pink
batts fit among studs of

bone, friction, light
across all this the

body's heat
itching at the spun

beauty, at the empty and
translucent room

vi

Shovel

the air unravels, smoke
wound among aerials and wire
and someone is burning coal
in their fireplace, you can
smell it
      though you cannot
say where it comes from.
it is in the air, diffuse
as light, late this afternoon
a day lengthening perceptibly
now, the end
of January
        and you have
cleared the sidewalks
again, sweating, short of
breath among
predicted snow

Cross-country

because it is warmer than you
thought and you brought the
wrong wax and overdressed

and because it was the first time
out this season and you
haven't kept in shape

and your boots felt stiff
and your breath hurt and your
arms were sore from holding

you up so often.   because
the kids went by you
uphill.   because skidoos

which you still hear
snarling in the valley
chewed the trail up, tho signs

were posted to keep them
out.   because the air
is crystal, the chickadee

you stopped to watch, or
so you explained it,
circled the dry

trunk, head
in the bark, eyes hard with light.
because

there is a need for exercise,
beauty, the heart
nothing but itself,

its urgency, circling,
the skiers across the valley
stride evenly

viii

Cocoa butter

I would never have recognized it
but I saw the jar
beside the bed.

I don't want
                    anything.

Your skin glows.

ix

Wind chill

the air's lustre, what
it does with light

as a nickel, held, between
thumb and forefinger
is warmed
for no reason

only that the hand
closes
as it does

and it is lost, the nickel,
glowing, in loose snow

Après-ski

i

nobody
is more lonely
than the driver

of a car full of sleepers
coming home from a trip
to the mountains

they fold their jackets into
pillows and lean on one another
and never crowd the driver

night bends on the highway, full
of snow, static
for the radio, a place

to fill with light, and the
sleepers, dreaming, their
feet hot, wake

and ask, how
much further

ii

even sleeping a body is not perfect
of itself

they lie on their bruises
and have to move.   it's like that:

you drive they said, and we'll
keep you awake

now
their throats get sore, the soft
rasp of nylon against
nylon, plastic zippers

the small
movements of a body finding
comfort, leaning
in an enclosed space

against the drift of other
bodies
against the door

iii

snow in the headlights

blind transparent fish
that glow in pools
in the belly of the rock

you strike a match
and they come gaping

to the surface

iv

green of dashlights.   the wheel
    tugs in his hands.
                          out
        of the mountains, the car
            dreams direction.

moonlight, fields of shallow water, her
    hand falling, accidently,
        in his lap

            all misread: body
            moon, horizon, the
                hand not held

        and his legs, sleeping
            because he will not move them

v

it is the accidental
the lapse, that keeps
him awake.   after

so many miles the light
is all glare.   traffic
glows like fish

he has only imagined
black pools under the
mountain

they wake in the city
the light, or the rhythm
gone, and say

you must be tired
are we here already

and disappear
into the dark house, with
skis, boots, half-empty
cases of beer, the way

fish
disappear in rock

vi

days later

it swims in them, the stiffness
the brilliant snow, all the ways
of recollection

held
like coffee mugs in a tiny kitchen

you could've switched off
if you were tired
they tell him

his cup is full of settled
grounds
remembered
into his hand

as any
plan
made, an
aching in the legs

he says he doesn't really mind
the driving and

reaches out
to be filled again

My wife paints her fingers

i

loner. a bandit sneaks
up on a crowd. in the suburbs
of the hand he goes quietly
insane. she should paint
a mask across his eye.
when you make a gun with
your fingers he's the hammer.

ii

when your fingers do the walking
he walks. let's wobble this job.
he leans against the lips
like the unemployed at a wicket.
he was looking for a job
when he found this one.
he touches the dial of a phone
the way he touches the body's
gossip. kiss and tell.
in the bar-rooms of the nose
he points you out and talks
up union. he loves a profit
margin the way he never
loved you.

iii

regal. a queen in front
of the bastard's firing squad.
her ladies lean on her
for support and protection.
she says vive la france and fuck you.
when they drop a hood
over her head you still
can feel her eyes.

iv

the one most given away. she
sneaks out of the castle
in golden slippers and tries
to lose herself in the crowd.
but nothing can hide the beauty
or the lust. sometimes she
can't give it away.
paint her red and she's embarrassed.

v

at the end of the table
dissent. a little left
wing. the standing committee
agree and they nod their heads
this year its the blue-reds
they smoulder and she blows
on them and they smoulder.
but this minority.
holds out the way skin
holds out on the lips
and then gives in.

Mysteries of the Great Plains

from the book by Monty Reid

i

What Immediate Effect did the Great Plains have upon the Anglo-Saxons?

Fragile. Morning hangs in the valley, among damp clumps of aspen, trembling. Figures move along high bluffs, indistinct in the river mist, carrying canoes, bundles wrapped in rope and leather thongs. The trail is filmed with frost; treacherous. Below them water shatters in a throat of stones. Their mouths are taut. At the rear of the party is a man with a cocked hat and a sextant. Behind him are two Indians carrying a stretcher. There, wrapped in swaths of frost-stiffened furs, his fingers clutching a notebook, lies an incapacitated Peter Fidler. He has sore feet. A disquieting odour of bitumen is rafted through the valley on the fog.

Did Man Originate on the Plains or in the Forest?

At their dig, where they have successfully recovered the skeleton of an animal previously unrecorded in this country, the palaeontologists are having a party. They stand, in gowns and black tie, beside a fire on the pebbled flats of the valley. Some friends whom they have not seen for a long time have come down from the city for the occasion. Canvas tents are pitched in the shadows at the base of the valley wall. Between the tents and the river are piled like discarded styrofoam the bones of the old animal wrapped in plaster of paris. A barge is lying in the river. Firelight licks between the slats of crates stacked on the barge. As the palaeontologists toast each other and their most recent find the rope slowly unravels. And the barge floats out of the light in the slow disentangling of the river.

iii

Why is the West considered Spectacular and Romantic?

On the front porch sit an aluminum ladder, some asphalt shingles, batts of insulation and a pair of muddy boots. Rain is being driven in through open windows. The bundles of shingles have been thrown on the batts of insulation to prevent them from blowing away. Although they have been placed as far from the window as possible, the boots have filled with water.

Two young women come out of the house onto the porch. They are wearing laced camisoles and they throw themselves, laughing, upon the insulation, wrenching handfuls of fibreglas from the wet batts. When they embrace they place a batt of fibreglas between them. They take the shingles off the insulation and the wind lifts the batts across the porch like helpless birds. The women wad fibreglas into their mouths and slide the ladder out the window.

*Why was the West considered Lawless? Was it really Lawless or
did it merely Appear Lawless?*

The Saskatchewan Roughriders are running through offensive
drills on the prairie southeast of Calgary. It is an away game.
There are no yardsticks or hash marks. They are trying to get their
timing down. After every play the coaches, one of whom stands in
front of the centre, the second slightly behind and to the left of the
setbacks, can be seen writing vigorously in their notebooks. A
crowd has gathered at the roadside several hundred yards away,
watching through binoculars. There is no sound except the slap of
plastic on plastic, muffled in flesh. They are operating out of an I
formation. The quarterback has called a slant off left tackle. He
gives to the second man through. For an instant, a gaping hole is
created in the line and the back slashes into it. The defence is nowhere to be seen.

v

Why is the West politically Radical?

The train is carrying a load of green lumber to Toronto. Somewhere, a spark has escaped from an overheated bearing, setting the plastic that wraps the stacks of plywood and 2x4s, masonite and chipboard, ablaze. Although the wood is green, it burns fiercely. It is midnight. The train drags a plume of fire across the flat land, the lumber warping in the heat, sap oozing from the planks, boiling. 2x4s spill off the car, tumbling over and over through the autumn fields like the rigid legs of huge metallic insects. Plywood rips off the stacks, settling in sheets of flame upon the swaths. When the train stops at the next town the burnt cars are unhooked and left to smoulder at the siding. The town does not have a fire department. It has been named after G.U. Ryley, once a surveyor for the CNR.

In Conclusion, let us inquire what has been and what is to be the Meaning of the Great Plains in American Life?

On the wall of the living room is a velvet painting of a covered wagon in the desert. There is a huge copper sun in the top left corner of the picture. Spikes of weathered rock cast shadows in an unmistakeable profile onto the canvas. As if there was a face behind the painting. When she got her divorce she left this piece with her parents because there was no room in her small apartment. They said someday you'll want it back but she has forgotten. The dust from the covered wagon, painted with a vigor apparent nowhere else in the painting, coats almost everything.

Yield

i

it was a beautiful crop and there was
a track through it so we followed it.

she broke heads off the stalks and rubbed
them into her palm. green kernels fell out.

she put them, one by one, into her mouth.

ii

at night, combines
in the field, a low
moon, the smell
of stubble

she waited in the truck
hot coffee, a blanket
on her legs

the radio on, softly
a song about bright
lights, some distant
city

      she once
would have given
anything, the acres
of stars, as though
they were hers

    to give

    to see

iii

watch how fields make the air

move
how they lean up to hold the wind

how heat quivers over them

watch how a path is made
the wheat bent
over

how a path
needs two people, a crop so full
and high there is nothing in it except
harvest, how a path needs no
direction

watch she said

the chaff swirled in her palm

I hold up my hand
and the wind

comes to it

iv

we had a blue
blanket

do you know how
to make gum

she said

The pictures of Williams

i

on the New Directions
printing of
Imaginations

light blocked
across taut skin
what is known
of cartilage, the
moral odors
veins flex at
the temple in
the shadow of
the whole right
side
the lips are
a flat line
the hair
springs away
eyebrows down
dark above dark eyes
looking at some
thing

ii

unposed
        you can tell
because
        he is facing right
               it
is the first time
        he stands
             like that
Flossie is there
        she
has a pigeon
        in her hand

p. 125 of
Adrift Among Geniuses

iii

1st photo in *William Carlos Williams* by Laurette Veza

one photo par
Man Ray
        Williams
has a scarf
it is winter and
the man is well
kempt
        he is grey
or thinning at
the temples why
does he always
look that direction
it is winter
                he has
just come
from the baroness you
can tell

iv

3rd photo in Veza book

for once
he looks
off to my left
his right there
is nothing
there I am
in Rutherford
Library it's
two thirty
this picture
was taken for
Random House

V

the face is
not so round the
eyes hooded or half
hooded anyway
in 1926
he was an
impatient man
Charles Scheeler
took this one
the chair is full
of holes   his hands
balance together
and he is eager
to get up
the diagnosis
is clarity here
of the best

vi

on the New Directions
printing of
The Farmers' Daughters

above the city
that might be Paterson
he still looks
off to the left
although the hair
is white the lines
are the same
but this time the hands
or one hand covering
the other, the blunt
nails the doctor
clips and keeps
at the edge of the
picture behind him
the city is alive

vii

well
rounded   he
looks like a retired
president
        Roosevelt maybe
the man on the
pillar that gives
vertical dimension
behind him
he has his bow
tie on crooked
as he walks out
of the square

2nd photo in
Veza book

viii

on the New Directions
printing of
Selected Poems

he looks like my
                    grandmother
the face still
                    looking
the same way
                    the same lines
only more
          the neck
                    looks thin
he has a straw
                    hat as if
he had just
                    come from the garden

Bunker sonnets

i

Nothing changed.
                    The doors
closed, ashes settle, you hear them
almost, the way you hear a forest
slump into darkness late in summer.

Survivors are full of metaphor, a
dream of seasons, winter, spring,
the rest of them.   Already
there are those convinced
nothing happened.
                              Concrete.
          Lead.
                    The mind hums with
something like seasons.

ii

all their bodies left were shadows
burnt into what was left of walls

all their bodies left was vapor
cracking in what was left of air

all their bodies left was a roar
of fire, the air sucked in and held

a breath over the city
all their bodies left was the exhaled
light

all I have left for the dead
is contempt

iii

it was not a secret because we
kept it.   this shelter.   no one
took it.   it was as if we whispered
into the ear of the city and the city
said so what.   fuck, you'd have to hit
them with a stick to wake them up.

three places: under city hall, under
police headquarters, under the post office
only the last hardened.   when
we filed in no one was there
except the cops and they were bored.
so why remember.
                           because
we are all perfected and alive.
because in two weeks we'll all
come out and listen
to the secrets
in the air

iv

recirculated air

stale, as
if the dead
were in it
             in
          the air

     I have breathed before
        so thick I can see
     my teethmarks in it

somewhere: filters, charcoal,
          water, fibreglas, chemicals
               someone is familiar with

     somewhere   someone

          me   here

          chewing my knuckles

v

to pass the time — poker

we invent so much to lose:
    home, shop, wife
        goes with the house

how we imagine we have everything
and bet it on our hands

there were parties I remember
coming home from

with change in my pockets
and dawn starting to slide
into things...
            all the words
            take me outside...

    like those first steps
        when there is nothing left
        nothing more that can be imagined

        when the glow dies
and morning is steady in the ashes

vi

i jerk-off because it is the only
way to remember you

or because it is the only way to forget

i can't tell the difference
only that it takes
longer and longer

i want every thing to be said, not
suggested, not left to my imagination

say your name

say love

say waterbed

say you will never forget me

o christ, i know the details:
your shoulders, how your bra
left red marks, the small scar
low on your back
                    turn over

i jerk off to keep from talking

vii

perhaps we are the dead and all
the rest go mad in their certainty.
mad and alive.   perhaps
there was no bomb.

perhaps we had bad advice.
perhaps we played into the hands
of our enemies.   now that it confounds us
we ache for knowledge.

the way our feet ache on the concrete
and everyone has piles

sure it's funny

perhaps there are no dead

viii

we go dull as lead, as re-bar
twisted in broken concrete.

too dull for envy.

the flat gunmetal of guilt
the stubborn rhetoric
gone blind in our heads:

that there is a coming out
that we want to be dead
that we will blame
ourselves
all that bullshit

as though this bunker were
thought
         merely

the radiant abstract mind, not
    a hole under the slowest
        post office in the world

ix

say the world

say winter, spring, the runoff
seeping through our lawn towards
the alley.   stamps.   football scores.
blue jay in the snow.

all those things made
        of our love
                        our failure
                        to be silent

        the ordinary dying of our cells

    only those who are safe
        have nothing left

                        to say

The dream of snowy owls

i

Slow wings. The arrival
late in October, of snow.
It begins and you have
never learned to expect it
because nothing changes
fast enough. Love,
wisdom, weather.
Owl on a pole

From the overpass north to the beaverdam is eight miles of meander, deadfall. They got up and put a hard white wax on their skis and broke trail up the creek. Moonlit snow. Stitched by shadow from the bare willow branches. Once they heard an owl and stopped. Twice they found the end of tracks. Shit, green bark in the scrub, rosehips with a faint red still in them like wineglasses left on the night-table, gnawed. The rabbit flushed, then wings.

They remembered angels. How they fell into fresh snow backwards and tried to get up and walk away in their old footprints. No unnecessary marks. But now sweat glues everything to them, layered clothing, the quilted snow, and they need motion to release them. Shivering, they turn towards the overpass, going back as snow comes in through gaps in black poplar along the bank, flakes collapsing as petals collapse off the cherry tree in their garden, not in a hard frost but in the sunlight afterwards. Two miles out she broke a tip and had to walk the rest of the way.

iii

he rarely dreams
    but dreams owls.   fixed eyes.   snow
        on the highway.

          they refuse to move, perched
on shattered roadkill with intestines
    in their beaks, the brown
      bands deep across
        breast and wing
   not the immaculate birds of midwinter
    but spring, the hollow
      bones brooding with instinct

   ready to fly
        north.

driving, he would brake, swerve, barely
  miss them
    and they were indifferent

   the first one he hit hardly moved.
he did not think to look back.

   but they walked under the wheels, owl
    after owl, feathers, pillows
      broken
          an airless room
   and in his hands, no feeling
he would peer in the mirror
   and discover them whole
            unruffled
        pivoting their heads
         to watch him
           disappear.

in the end it was deliberate.   steering
    at them, his foot rammed
with belief against the floor.
    he rarely dreams and when he does
        the dreams wake him.

    moonlight
                sheers

        frost

    unfolded
                on the glass

iv

in the summer they are gone.
he sleeps with the window
open and sweats into the pillow.
in the school library, an owl
mounted on a cut maple, a patch
of rabbit fur in its talons.
the librarian cannot remember
who donated it.

v

early March, driving
home from the city
in a wet snow, an

owl, caught in the solid
light, lifted
so slowly from the shoulder

no feather, no
wing, just a thud
on the glass, an imagined

flailing behind him now
tho he returned to
look, the snow

melting
inaudibly
on the pavement

vi

undreamt, the owl
flies from the pole
or does not fly
                    that
there are wings, silent,
held, among curtains, glass,
a body of light persistent
in snow, a particular
symmetry

that the owl, at
least, assumes air
and the air
embraces it